I0425874

April 2012

ENERGY CONSERVATION AND CLIMATE CHANGE

Factors to Consider in the Design of the Nonbusiness Energy Property Credit

Contents

Letter		1
	Scope and Methodology	2
	Summary	3
	Agency Comments	4
Appendix I	Briefing Slides	5
Appendix II	Use of the Credit by Spending Categories and Limits	32

Abbreviations

AGI	adjusted gross income
CO_2	carbon dioxide
DOE	Department of Energy
IRC	Internal Revenue Code
IRS	Internal Revenue Service
SOI	Statistics of Income Database

United States Government Accountability Office
Washington, DC 20548

April 2, 2012

The Honorable Max Baucus
Chairman
Committee on Finance
United States Senate

The Honorable Jeff Bingaman
United States Senate

The Honorable Dianne Feinstein
United States Senate

The Honorable John F. Kerry
United States Senate

The Honorable Olympia J. Snowe
United States Senate

The nonbusiness energy property credit[1] is one of a number of federal initiatives that seek to address concerns about U.S. reliance on foreign energy sources and the impact of carbon dioxide (CO_2) emissions on the climate. Enacted as part of the Energy Policy Act of 2005, the nonbusiness energy property credit was intended to increase homeowners' investment in energy conserving improvements by reducing their after-tax costs. The credit is calculated as a percentage of qualified spending on such improvements as insulation systems, exterior windows and metal roofs up to a maximum claimable credit. The maximum credit was set at $500 in 2006 and 2007, raised to $1,500 in 2009 and 2010, and lowered back to $500 in 2011.

In the enclosed slides, this report compiles and expands upon information previously presented to you in response to your request, which asked us to examine factors relating to the nonbusiness energy property credit. To address the request, we (1) evaluated factors to consider in deciding whether the credit should be cost-based or performance-based; and (2) estimated how requiring that only spending above a minimum amount be

---

[1] I.R.C. § 25C.

eligible for the credit, or introducing a base amount for the 2009 credit may have affected measures such as the amount of credit claimed, the revenue cost to the federal government, and incentives for taxpayers to increase their spending on energy efficiency improvements.

Scope and Methodology

For our first objective—to evaluate factors to consider in deciding whether the credit should be cost-based or performance-based—we reviewed relevant literature and consulted with experts on criteria for a well-designed credit. On the basis of this review, we determined that tax credit design, which includes such factors as whether the credit is cost-based or performance-based, should be evaluated according to:

- how well the logic of the design is related to the credit's purpose,
- how likely the design is to achieve that purpose,
- how costly it would be to achieve this purpose using this design, and
- how fairly the credit's costs and benefits are distributed under this design.

Using these criteria, we analyzed the current credit and changes that have been proposed to it.

For our second objective—estimating how introducing a base spending amount for the 2009 credit may have affected measures such as the amount of credit claimed, the revenue cost to the federal government, and incentives for taxpayers to increase their spending on energy efficiency improvements—we used the Internal Revenue Service's (IRS) 2009 Statistics of Income (SOI) database, the most current data available, to simulate the effects that different bases would have had on credit claimed, revenue costs, and incentives faced by taxpayers, using actual spending and purchase patterns from the 2009 credit claims. These simulations do not include behavioral responses such as changes in the number of claimants and amounts of spending due to the credit. To conduct these simulations, we examined two alternative bases: a base calculated as a percentage of adjusted gross income (AGI) and a base derived from average spending on different types of improvements. For this objective, we reviewed documentation for the databases we used, conducted electronic checks, and determined that the data presented were sufficiently reliable for our purposes.

Throughout this report, the percentage estimates have a margin of error of plus or minus 5 percentage points, and the estimates of total amounts have a margin of error of plus or minus 5 percent of the estimate.

We conducted this performance audit from August 2010 to April 2012 in accordance with generally accepted government auditing standards. Those standards require that we plan and perform the audit to obtain sufficient, appropriate evidence to provide a reasonable basis for our findings and conclusions based on our audit objectives. We believe that the evidence obtained provides a reasonable basis for our findings based on our audit objectives.

Summary

Under criteria for evaluating a tax credit design, both the performance-based and cost-based credits have advantages and disadvantages with neither design being unambiguously the better option based on current information. Both a cost-based and a performance-based credit are designed to reduce energy use and CO_2 emissions by providing incentives for energy conservation investment. However, they differ in their relative effectiveness and costs. In general, a performance-based credit is more likely to effectively reduce energy use and CO_2 emissions because it rewards energy savings from the investment rather than the cost-based credit's rewarding of spending regardless of whether this spending results in energy savings. However, the performance-based credit may have significant up-front costs for energy audits, not required by the cost-based credit, which could reduce its effectiveness by discouraging investment. In addition, for taxpayers who do invest, these up-front costs may mean that a performance-based credit may have significantly higher taxpayer compliance and IRS administrative costs than a cost-based credit. A credit's fairness depends on subjective judgments of how a credit varies with a taxpayer's income level.

For those taxpayers claiming the 2009 credit, under both base definitions used in our simulations, the total amount of credit claimed fell but taxpayers had a greater incentive to spend more on qualifying products. The incentive was measured as the average effective rate of credit that would apply to additional spending by taxpayers. In 2009, when no base was present, a dollar of additional spending would earn, on average, an additional 10 cents of credit. When the base derived from average spending was introduced in the simulations, a dollar of additional spending earned an estimated 14 to 18 cents of credit. However, because the simulations do not include behavioral responses, the overall effect on revenues and spending of introducing a base is uncertain. For example, introducing a base amount, while likely to limit windfall credits for qualified spending that would have been done anyway, would also make the credit less generous and some taxpayers might no longer use it.

We are not making new recommendations based on this review. This work is intended to assist Congress in considering different ways that the credit can be structured to achieve the stated goals of reducing CO_2 emissions and minimizing U.S. reliance on foreign energy sources.

Agency Comments

The Internal Revenue Service, the Department of Energy, and the Department of the Treasury provided us with technical comments after viewing a draft of this report, which we incorporated as appropriate.

Unless you publicly announce the contents of this report earlier, we plan no further distribution until 30 days from the date of this letter. At that time we will send copies of this report to other Chairmen and Ranking Members of Senate and House committees and subcommittees that have appropriation and oversight responsibilities for IRS. We also will be sending copies to the Commissioner of Internal Revenue, the Secretary of the Treasury, and the Secretary of Energy. Copies are also available at no charge on the GAO Web site at http://www.gao.gov.

Should you or your staff have questions concerning this report, please contact me at (202) 512-6806 or mihmj@gao.gov. Key contributors to this report were Michael Brostek, Director; Kevin E. Daly, Assistant Director; Susan F. Baker; Sara Daleski; Lawrence M. Korb; Jeffrey Schmerling; Albert Sim; Ardith A. Spence; and Anne O. Stevens.

J. Christopher Mihm
Managing Director
Strategic Issues

Energy Conservation and Climate Change:

Factors to Consider in the Design of
the Nonbusiness Energy Property
Tax Credit

Introduction

- Various federal initiatives have sought to address concerns about U.S. reliance on foreign energy sources and the impact of carbon dioxide (CO_2) emissions on the climate.

- One initiative is the nonbusiness energy property credit (I.R.C. §25C),[1] a tax credit that could encourage taxpayers to invest in residential energy efficiency improvements.

[1]Energy Policy Act of 2005, Pub. L. No. 109-58, § 1333, 119 Stat. 594 (Aug. 8, 2005).

2

Objectives

- To address questions about whether the nonbusiness energy property credit is the best or most effective way to encourage investment in energy efficiency improvements, GAO was asked to:
  - evaluate factors to consider in deciding whether the credit should be cost-based or performance-based, and

  - estimate how requiring that only spending above a minimum amount be eligible for the credit, or introducing a base amount for the 2009 credit may have affected measures such as the amount of credit claimed, the revenue cost to the federal government, and incentives for taxpayers to increase their spending on energy efficiency improvements.
- We were also asked for information on use of the credit by spending categories and limits. This information is contained in appendix II.

Summary

- Both the performance-based and cost-based credits have advantages and disadvantages with neither design being unambiguously the better option given current information.
  - The performance-based credit rewards energy savings from the investment rather than, as is the case with the cost-based credit, the spending on investment whether this spending results in energy savings or not.
  - However, the performance-based credit may have significant up-front costs for energy audits, not required by the cost-based credit, which could reduce its effectiveness by discouraging investment and increase its compliance and administrative costs relative to the cost-based credit.
- Under both base definitions used in our simulations, the total amount of credit claimed fell and taxpayers who were already investing in qualifying purchases had a greater incentive to spend more.
  - For example, in 2009, when no base was present, a dollar of additional spending would earn, on average, an additional 10 cents of credit, but when we simulated a base derived from average spending, a dollar of additional spending would earn on average an estimated 14 to 18 cents of credit.
  - However, because the simulations do not include behavioral responses, including the decision to make any initial investment, the overall effect on revenues and spending of introducing a base is uncertain.

4

Background—2006 and 2007 Credit

- Enacted as part of the Energy Policy Act of 2005,[2] the nonbusiness energy property credit was intended to increase homeowners' investment in energy conserving improvements by reducing their after-tax costs.

  - In 2006 and 2007, the maximum claimable credit was $500.
    - Of this $500, a maximum of $200 could be claimed on exterior windows
    - In all years, any credit amounts exceeding tax liability could not be carried forward.

  - The credit was calculated as 10 percent of qualified spending on insulation systems, exterior windows, exterior doors, and metal roofs.

  - Spending on other types of residential energy property received a 100 percent credit but had credit limits by spending category, specifically:
    - up to $50 for advanced main air circulating fans used in a furnace;
    - up to $150 for furnaces or hot water boilers; and
    - up to $300 for heat pumps, central air conditioning systems, or water heaters.

[2] Pub. L. No. 109-58, § 1333, 119 Stat. 594 (Aug. 8, 2005).

5

Background (Cont.)—2009 Credit

- After expiring in 2008, the credit was reauthorized for 2009 and 2010 as part of the American Recovery and Reinvestment Tax Act of 2009

    - the overall credit limit was raised from $500 to $1,500;

    - the rate of credit, which in 2006 and 2007 varied based on the type of spending, was set at 30 percent for all types of qualified spending; and

    - credit limits by spending category were eliminated.

- For 2011, the credit was reauthorized at pre-Recovery Act limits and standards.

6

GAO-12-318 Nonbusiness Energy Property Tax Credit

Background (Cont.)—Taxpayer Characteristics:

Number of claimants, total credit claimed, and total spending in 2006, 2007, and 2009

- In 2006 and 2007, over 4 million taxpayers claimed the credit, and in 2009, the number of claimants increased to almost 7 million.

- From 2006 to 2007, both spending and credit claimed declined, but in 2009, compared to 2007 levels, the total spending more than tripled and the credit claimed increased five-fold.

- The increase in total spending in 2009 may be explained in part by a change in the relevant tax form's instructions, which did not limit the amount the claimant could enter on the form for categories that were previously subject to limits.

Table 1: Total Returns Filed, Claimants, Spending, and Credit Claimed for the Nonbusiness Energy Property Credit, 2006, 2007, and 2009[3]

Year	Total tax returns filed (millions)	Total claimants (millions)	Total spending (millions of dollars)[a]	Total credit claimed (millions of dollars)
2006	138.4	4.3	$7,947	$956
2007	153.6[b]	4.3	$7,484	$938
2009	140.5	6.8	$25,567	$5,288

Source: GAO analysis of IRS data.

[a]Spending reported to IRS in 2006 and 2007 could not exceed certain category limits; for 2009, no category limits were included in the reporting instructions.

[b]For 2007, the aggregate number of returns include those returns that were filed solely to receive an economic stimulus payment. Excluding these returns, 143.0 million returns were filed in 2007.

[3]GAO estimates were computed using the SOI advance 2009 Individual Complete Report. In our computations, the nonbusiness energy property credit is applied against tax liability remaining after all other credits are taken into account.

Current Design:
Elements of Both a Cost- and Performance-Based Credit

- Cost-based credits provide incentives that are usually a fixed percentage of qualified spending, or sometimes, qualified spending above a base amount.

- Performance-based credits provide incentives that are tied to specific measures of energy savings.

- The nonbusiness energy property credit combines features of both cost-based and performance-based credits.
    - It is cost-based in that the amount of credit claimed is directly proportional to the taxpayer's qualified spending.
    - It is performance-based in that only certain qualifying purchases are eligible.

Design Evaluation:
Both performance- and cost-based credits are designed to conserve energy and reduce CO_2 emissions by subsidizing energy conservation investment

- The credit's purpose is to reduce inefficient energy consumption and CO_2 emissions.
    - The rationale for providing the tax credit is the view that individuals invest too little from society's point of view when they consider only their own energy cost savings.
    - In addition, there is evidence that taxpayers make too little energy conservation investment based on their own energy costs. They do this, for example, when they underestimate the savings from future operating cost reductions due to their more efficient equipment.
- Both the cost- and performance-based credits address this purpose by providing incentives for energy conservation investment.[4]
    - Who actually benefits from the credit depends on its incidence, i.e., the share of the credit going to producers and consumers of the improvements. If supply is relatively unresponsive to price, a greater share of the benefit would go to producers in the form of higher prices. This result may still be consistent with the purpose of the credit if it promotes the growth of markets for more energy efficient products.
- Ideally, the credit should be designed to reduce individuals' costs sufficiently so that, in the aggregate, their return on investment equals society's return in terms of energy use and CO_2 emission reductions.

[4]While both credit designs address the purpose of the credit, they do so indirectly by promoting conservation investment. Another, more direct method of reducing energy use and CO_2 emissions that has been suggested is a carbon tax on energy consumption.

GAO-12-318 Nonbusiness Energy Property Tax Credit

Design Evaluation:
The performance-based credit better targets conservation investment but its higher initial costs may discourage some investment

- For a better chance of producing the intended benefit, the credit should target activities that most directly promote the credit's purpose and provide sufficient incentives for taxpayers to increase these activities.
- The performance-based credit is likely to better target conservation investment spending.
  - The performance-based credit provides fixed amounts of credit for achieving different levels of energy savings. It therefore provides an incentive for taxpayers to minimize the spending required to achieve a given amount of energy savings. The credit is designed to reward additional energy savings and CO_2 reductions but not additional spending.
  - The cost-based credit is designed to reward spending on conservation investment that may, or may not, lead ultimately to additional energy savings.
- However, the relative effectiveness of the incentives provided by performance-based and cost-based credits is less certain.
  - Performance based credits are likely to have larger up-front costs than cost-based credits and may discourage taxpayers from buying qualifying energy savings products.
    - These costs include energy audits to establish a baseline of energy use against which to measure improvements and possibly post-improvement audits to confirm that energy savings have been realized. These added costs could reduce the incentive to undertake any investments.
    - On the other hand, such audits might also increase participation if they reassure taxpayers that they will actually save energy.

10

Design Evaluation:
Performance-based credits may have significantly higher compliance and administrative costs than cost-based credits

- To assess the credit design, the benefits likely to be produced by the credit should be compared to its costs, which include the lost tax revenue and IRS administrative costs as well as more indirect costs, such as taxpayer compliance burden and economic efficiency costs.

- Performance-based credits may have significantly higher compliance and administrative costs than cost-based credits.
  - Taxpayer compliance costs are higher due to up-front costs, such as energy audits not required by cost-based credits.
  - According to IRS officials, administration costs are likely to be higher for performance-based credits that reward measurable (not estimated) increases in energy efficiency because examinations would have to verify that improvements were made, not just that money was spent.

- The relative economic efficiency costs of the alternative credit designs are uncertain because their effects depend on the degree to which the credits alter decisions to spend across different improvement types and how much they reduce energy use and CO_2 emissions. The effects are difficult to infer from design alone.

- The relative effect of a cost-based credit and performance-based credit on revenue costs is uncertain because it depends chiefly on whether the credit has base amounts and limits and which credit rates are chosen.

11

Design Evaluation:
The fairness of how the credit's costs and benefits are distributed depends on subjective value judgments

- The fairness of the credit's design depends on the judgment of whoever is evaluating the design.
  - Views on what is a fair distribution of the credit's costs and benefits can differ dramatically across individuals.
- However, whatever one's views of fairness, an analysis of the distribution of costs and benefits by such factors as income level can be useful.
- Under an ability to pay principle of fairness, fairness requires that those who are more capable of bearing the burden of a tax should pay more. Equivalently, for a tax credit, they should receive less of the benefit.
  - Those who adopt an ability-to-pay principle of fairness may view as unfair a distribution where lower income taxpayers receive lower benefits from the credit than higher income taxpayers.
- However, under the same principle, fairness requires that taxpayers who have the same ability to pay should bear the same tax burden, or in this case, receive the same benefit.
  - Those who adopt this principle may view as unfair that taxpayers who invest in energy conservation have lower tax liabilities than taxpayers with the same income who do not invest.

12

Introducing a Base:
Credit Design Features

- As currently designed, all qualified spending up to the various limits is eligible for the nonbusiness energy property credit. This design increases the likelihood of windfall credits being earned for spending on qualifying energy efficient investments that would have occurred without the credit.

- A base that would eliminate windfall benefits would reward only the additional spending that taxpayers make due to the availability of the credit.
  - The credit amount would be calculated as the credit rate multiplied by the amount of qualified spending in excess of the base amount.
  - A base that eliminates windfalls is difficult to determine because it requires estimating how much consumers would spend on the types of products qualifying for the credit if the credit did not exist.
  - Because such a base amount is difficult to determine, other tax credits, such as the research tax credit, use proxies for these unknown amounts.

Introducing a Base:
Effects on the Use of the Credit

- Introducing a base can affect use of the credit in two opposite ways:
  - The base can reduce the take-up rate of the credit, i.e., the number of taxpayers making qualifying purchases.
    - Because the amount of credit on spending only over a base amount generally would be less than a credit on the full amount of spending on a qualifying purchase, some taxpayers may choose to make no investment at all.
    - Several factors could affect the taxpayers' decision to invest, such as the amount of spending that is "reactive," reflecting investment that cannot be postponed because of, for example, equipment failure.
  - The base can increase the amount of spending on qualifying purchases by those who choose to invest.
    - For those who have made the decision to invest, i.e., who are "in the market," the base can increase the incentive for additional spending.
      - In particular, claimants constrained by credit limits (about 25 percent of claimants in 2009) may find that more of any additional spending will be eligible for the credit.
- The simulations in this report focus on this second effect and do not include the effects on spending due to any change in the number of taxpayers choosing to make an investment.

14

Introducing a Base:
Determining the Base

- Bases or floors that are currently part of the Internal Revenue Code include amounts calculated as a percentage of income (such as the floor on deductions for medical expenses) or spending (such as the research tax credit).
- Following this precedent in the code, the base for the nonbusiness energy property credit could be calculated as a percentage of each taxpayer's qualified spending or adjusted gross income (AGI).
  - This option could reduce the administrative costs of the base because it uses only the information reported on tax returns.[5]
- The base could also be calculated using price information on nonqualifying improvements.
  - The rationale is that such prices may be used to better approximate the spending that the taxpayer would have done without the credit.
  - Department of Energy (DOE) currently collects information on the costs of many types of energy efficient home improvements.
  - However, DOE indicates that because prices vary so widely across locations, it would be very difficult to construct a base from these prices that would apply nationally.
  - Setting bases that vary by location and product type would increase the administrative costs of the credit.

[5]the actual spending on qualifying investments would need to be calculated by IRS from information on prior tax year returns.

15

Introducing a Base:
The Base Used in the Simulations

- To illustrate the effects of introducing a base amount, we recalculated the amount of credit taxpayers would have claimed and estimated how incentives to use the credit would have changed under alternative base definitions, for the pattern of spending observed in 2009.
  - Percentage of AGI base: We calculated the AGI base as a percentage of the taxpayers' adjusted gross income where, for each category, this percentage was the average amount spent by claimants in 2009 as a share of their AGI.
  - Average spending base: We calculated the average spending base as the average of actual 2009 spending in each improvement category.
- It is not known how the credit take-up rate or spending would change if a base were introduced. We adjusted the base amount by a range of values--which we call the base rates--to show how sensitive our estimates of incentives and credit claimed are to the size of the base. The simulations used 25 percent, 50 percent, and 75 percent of these category bases as base rates.
  - When implementing a base, policymakers may wish to consider trade-offs between take-up rates and incentives for induced spending. All else equal, a lower base may have a less discouraging effect on the decision to invest but is more likely to reward spending that would have been done anyway.
- The simulations were run using the 2009 IRS Statistics of Income (SOI) database of individual tax returns and show what credit would have been claimed and other results if the different bases had been in effect. The comparison of the results of the simulations to the actual 2009 data shows the effects of introducing the bases.

16

Introducing a Base:
Illustration of How to Calculate Credits Using the
Average Spending Base

- The graph on the next slide illustrates the calculation of the base amount for the average spending base.
  - The spending type in this example is windows and the amount of qualified spending is $4,000.
  - Average qualified spending for windows by all taxpayers in 2009 was $3,665.
  - The base amount was calculated using the lowest base rate as 25 percent of average spending which is equal to $916.
    - If this base were implemented, IRS would, based on the most recent tax return data available, provide taxpayers the base amount--taxpayers would not be expected to calculate this amount.
- The credit is calculated as the difference between the qualified spending of $4,000 and the base amount of $916, which is equal to $3,084, multiplied by the credit rate of 30 percent, or about $925 of credit.

17

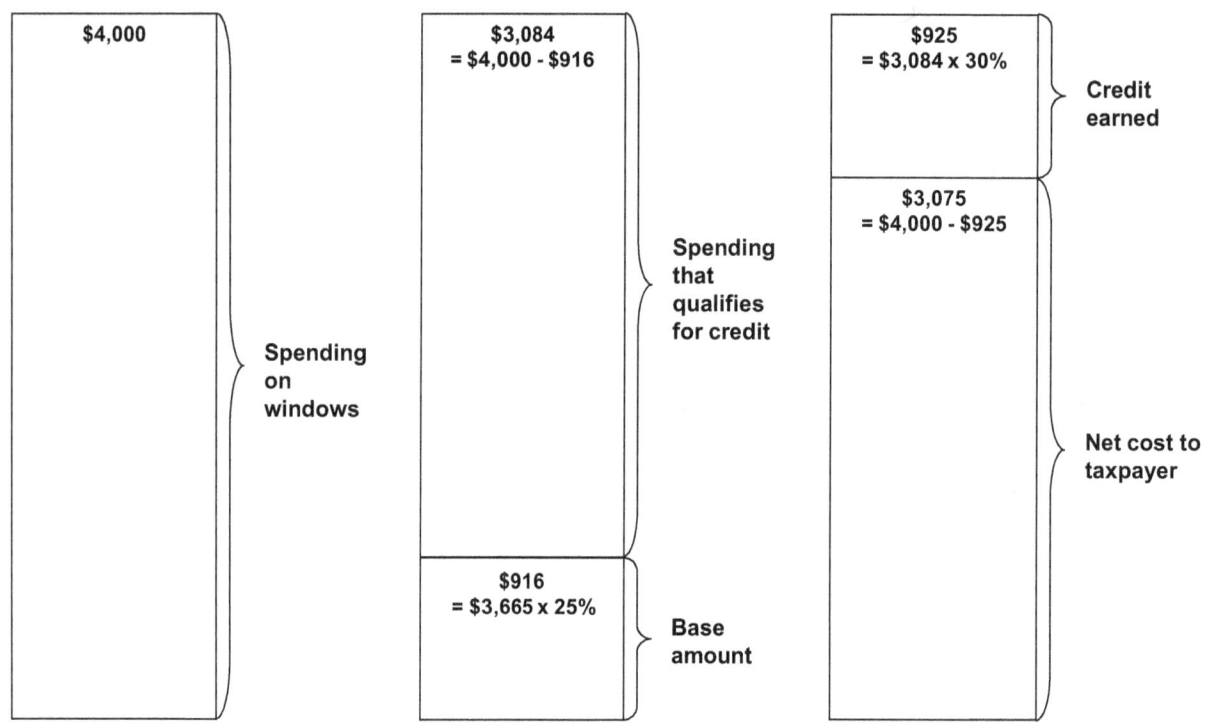

Introducing a Base: Illustrative Example of a Taxpayer Spending $4,000 on Windows (Average Spending Base)

Average spending base (average spending = $3,665; base rate = 25%)

18

Introducing a Base:
Illustration of How to Calculate Credits Using the Percentage of AGI Base

- The graph on the next slide illustrates the calculation of the base amount for the percentage of AGI base.
    - As in the previous example, the spending type is windows and the amount of qualified spending is $4,000.
    - AGI for this taxpayer is $25,000 and qualified spending on windows as an average share of income was about 5.1 percent in 2009.
    - The base amount for this taxpayer, using the lowest base rate of 25 percent, is equal to 1.275 percent of $25,000 of AGI (25 percent of the 5.1 percent share of income) which is equal to about $319.
        - If this base were implemented, taxpayers would be given the percentages corresponding to their level of AGI with their tax returns.
- The credit is the difference between the qualified spending of $4,000 and the base amount of $319, which is equal to $3,681, multiplied by the credit rate of 30 percent, or about $1,104 of credit.

19

Introducing a Base: Illustrative Example of a Taxpayer Spending $4,000 on Windows (AGI Base)

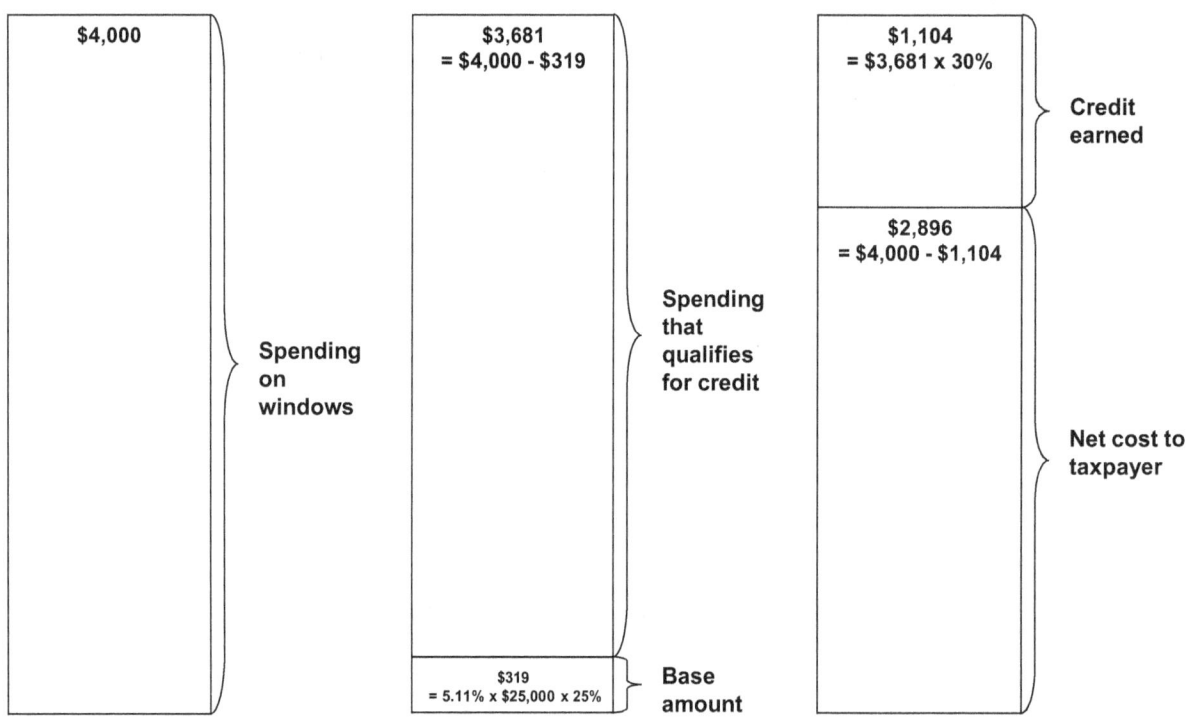

AGI base (average share of AGI spent = 5.11%; AGI = $25,000; base rate = 25%)

20

GAO-12-318 Nonbusiness Energy Property Tax Credit

Introducing a Base:
Illustration of Base Amounts, Qualified Spending, and Credit Amounts under Different Base Definitions and Base Rates

- The table on the next slide shows base spending and credit amounts for the average spending base under different assumptions about the base rates.

- The table also shows base, spending and credit amounts for the percentage of AGI base under different assumptions about the base rates and AGI.

- The total credit amount declines for both base types as the base rate increases.

- The credit amount for the percentage of income base decreases as income increases.
  - With the AGI base, a lower-income taxpayer will earn more credit than a higher income taxpayer spending the same amount. In the examples, the AGI base equals 5.11% of income multiplied by a base rate. For any base rate, the base amount increases as income rises so lower income taxpayers have a lower base. In the examples, taxpayers are assumed to spend $4,000 on windows, regardless of income, and the amount of spending that qualifies for credit is larger for lower-income taxpayers with a lower base.

21

GAO-12-318 Nonbusiness Energy Property Tax Credit

Introducing a Base: Illustrative Example of a Taxpayer Spending $4,000 on Windows

	Average spending base (average spending on windows in 2009 = $3,665)								
	Base amount (by base rate)			Spending qualifying for the credit (by base rate)			Credit earned (by base rate)		
	25%	50%	75%	25%	50%	75%	25%	50%	75%
	$916	$1,833	$2,749	$3,084	$2,168	$1,251	$925	$650	$375

Adjusted gross income base (average share of AGI spent on windows = 5.11 percent)

AGI	Base amount (by base rate)			Spending qualifying for the credit (by base rate)			Credit earned (by base rate)		
	25%	50%	75%	25%	50%	75%	25%	50%	75%
$25,000	$319	$639	$958	$3,681	$3,361	$3,042	$1,104	$1,008	$913
$75,000	$958	$1,916	$2,874	$3,042	$2,084	$1,126	$913	$625	$338
$150,000	$1,916	$3,833	$5,749	$2,084	$167	$0	$625	$50	$0

Source: GAO analysis of IRS data.

22

Introducing a Base:
Simulated Effects on Credit Claimed and Marginal Incentives in 2009 of Alternative Base Definitions

- In 2009, about $5.3 billion was claimed in nonbusiness energy property credit, and across all claimants the average marginal incentive was about 10 percent.
  - The average marginal incentive is the percentage change in the amount of credit associated with an increase or decrease in spending, divided by the percentage change in spending, averaged across all claimants.
  - In this case, on average, a dollar of additional spending would earn an additional 10 cents of credit, or equivalently, would reduce the cost of a dollar of additional spending by 10 cents.

- In simulations introducing a base spending amount, the amount of credit claimed fell, and the average marginal incentive to use the credit rose.
  - Introducing a base amount reduced the revenue cost of the credit to the government and simultaneously gave taxpayers a stronger incentive to invest in qualifying energy efficiency improvements.
  - Because the simulations do not include behavioral responses, the actual effect of introducing a base on revenues and spending is uncertain. Taxpayers facing a stronger incentive to use the credit may spend more than they otherwise would, increasing both the revenue cost of the credit and the amount spent on energy efficiency improvements. However, a base would also make the credit less generous overall, which could reduce the number of claimants, decreasing both the revenue cost of the credit and the amount spent on energy efficiency improvements.

Introducing a Base:
Simulated Effects on Credit Claimed and Marginal Incentives of Alternative Base Definitions in 2009

Base definition	2009 credit	Simulated credit with average spending base			Simulated credit with AGI base		
		Low–25 percent	Medium –50 percent	High–75 percent	Low–25 percent	Medium –50 percent	High–75 percent
Total credit earned (billions of dollars)	**5.3**	4.2	3.3	2.6	3.9	2.9	2.1
Average marginal incentive	**10%**	14%	16%	18%	15%	18%	21%

Source: GAO analysis of IRS data.

24

Introducing a Base:
Distributional Effects of the Alternative Bases

- Simulating a minimum spending requirement as a share of AGI indicates that taxpayers with between $0 and $80,000 in AGI would claim a larger share of the credit than they actually claimed in 2009. For example, in 2009, taxpayers with between $20,000 and $40,000 in AGI claimed about 10.2 percent of total credit. In simulations with an AGI base, they claimed from about 12.0 percent to about 16.3 percent of total credit, depending on the base rate.
  - Taxpayers with more than $100,000 in AGI generally accounted for a smaller share of credit claimed in simulations with an AGI base. For example, taxpayers with AGI between $250,000 and $500,000 claimed about 4.1 percent of credit in 2009 and between 1.5 and 2.9 percent of total credit in these simulations.
  - Under the AGI base, taxpayers with AGI between $80,000 and $100,000 accounted for about the same share of credit claimed as the share of credit they actually claimed in 2009.
- Simulating a base amount derived from average spending on qualifying purchases produced an opposite but less pronounced effect on the share of credit claimed by these income groups.
  - Taxpayers with AGI between $0 and $80,000 claimed a smaller share of credit than they actually claimed in 2009. For example, in simulations with an average spending base, taxpayers with between $20,000 and $40,000 in AGI claimed anywhere from about 8.1 percent to 9.4 percent of total credit, depending on the base rate, always less than the 10.2 percent of credit they claimed in 2009.
  - Taxpayers with AGI over $100,000 claimed a larger share of credit in simulations with an average spending base than they actually claimed in 2009. For example, taxpayers with AGI between $250,000 and $500,000 claimed between 4.6 and 5.6 of total credit in these simulations, as compared to 4.1 percent of total credit in 2009.

Introducing a Base:
Distributional Effects of the Alternative Bases

Adjusted gross income (dollars in thousands)	Percentage of all taxpayers with AGI > 0 in 2009	Share of credit claimed						
		2009	Simulated credit with an AGI base			Simulated credit with an average spending base		
			High	Medium	Low	High	Medium	Low
$0-$20	33.7%	0.8%	1.5%	1.2%	1.0%	0.6%	0.6%	0.7%
$20-$40	24.0	10.2	16.3	14.0	12.0	8.1	8.7	9.4
$40-$60	14.1	16.8	22.0	20.2	18.5	14.0	15.0	15.9
$60-$80	9.3	18.4	20.5	20.2	19.5	17.1	17.7	18.1
$80-$100	6.3	15.4	14.8	15.3	15.5	15.2	15.3	15.4
$100-$125	4.7	12.8	10.8	11.6	12.3	13.6	13.3	13.0
$125-$150	2.6	7.9	5.5	6.5	7.2	8.7	8.4	8.1
$150-$250	3.6	12.2	7.2	8.7	10.6	15.0	13.9	13.1
$250-$500	1.3	4.1	1.5	1.9	2.9	5.6	5.0	4.6
Greater than $500	0.5	1.5	0.2	0.3	0.5	2.2	1.9	1.7

Source: GAO analysis of IRS data.

26

GAO-12-318 Nonbusiness Energy Property Tax Credit

Conclusion

- The nonbusiness energy property credit has been claimed by millions of taxpayers since it was first introduced in 2006.

- While making the credit performance based likely would result in greater reductions in energy use than does the current credit, the performance based design is not clearly superior given current information because the performance-based credit likely would have greater taxpayer and government compliance and administration costs.

- If the cost-based credit is retained and a base spending amount was required, taxpayers who make qualifying purchases would have a greater incentive to spend more on such purchases and windfall benefits to those who would have made purchases without the credit would be reduced. However, a base spending requirement would reduce the absolute amount of credit taxpayers receive for qualifying purchases and might therefore result in fewer taxpayers making such purchases.

- Further, a base that excludes only windfall spending is difficult to construct. Proxy bases may over- or under correct for windfall benefits. A comprehensive evaluation of proxies for windfall spending would assess their effect on windfalls and their net effect on additional spending on qualified energy saving purchases.

27

GAO-12-318 Nonbusiness Energy Property Tax Credit

Appendix II: Use of the Credit by Spending Categories and Limits

28

Appendix II: Use of the Nonbusiness Energy Property Credit by Spending Categories and Limits

- About 5 million out of 6.8 million total claimants, or about 73 percent of all claimants, reported spending on only one type of energy improvement in 2009. Their qualified spending of about $16.7 billion accounts for about 65 percent of spending by all claimants.

- About 1.1 million of these claimants, or about 23 percent, were subject to the overall credit limit of $1,500, with close to 400,000 of these returns reporting spending on windows. About 6% of claimants reporting spending on only one type of improvement had limited tax liability that constrained the amount of credit claimed.

- A similar analysis of how spending was affected by limits for claimants reporting spending on more than one kind of improvement would be difficult. For instance, it is not possible to attribute their limited use of the credit to a particular category of spending, since constraints related to the overall credit limit or tax liability depend on total spending in all categories.

- The next three slides show the number of claimants and amount of spending by spending categories according to whether taxpayers were:
  - unconstrained by any of the credit's limits
  - constrained by the overall limit
  - constrained by the tax liability limit

29

Appendix II: Use of the Nonbusiness Energy Property Credit

Table 1: Use of the Nonbusiness Energy Property Credit by Unconstrained Claimants in 2009

Retrofit type	Claimants reporting spending on only one type of retrofit		Claimants reporting spending on more than one type of retrofit	
	Number	Spending (in millions)	Number	Spending (in millions)
Insulation	848,490	$947.0	644,100	$453.9
Windows	765,600	$1,605.2	619,284	$726.4
Doors	754,523	$811.3	681,297	$522.3
Roofs	107,659	$291.5	95,388	$136.2
Energy efficient building property	387,210	$875.1	132,373	$166.8
Furnaces and hot water boilers	608,467	$1251.0	214,217	$256.1
Furnace fans	52,218	$115.3	59,543	$57.2
All retrofit types	3,524,166	$5,896.3	1,060,682	$2,318.9

Source: GAO analysis of IRS data.

These tax returns account for about 68 percent of all claimants and about 32 percent of total spending in 2009. Because their use of the nonbusiness energy property credit is unconstrained, their credit claimed equals 30 percent of their spending, which is about 47 percent of all credit claimed.

30

Appendix II: Use of the Nonbusiness Energy Property Credit

Table 2: Use of the Nonbusiness Energy Property Credit by Claimants Subject to the Overall Credit Limit of $1,500 in 2009

Retrofit type	Claimants reporting spending on only one type of retrofit		Claimants reporting spending on more than one type of retrofit	
	Number	Spending (in millions)	Number	Spending (in millions)
Insulation	107,303	$850.8	281,604	$794.5
Windows	393,447	$3,635.8	425,030	$2,060.9
Doors	21,546	$160.2	319,995	$630.0
Roofs	86,786	$792.1	114,725	$676.5
Energy efficient building property	245,143	$1,944.9	139,584	$688.7
Furnaces and hot water boilers	237,430	$1,810.5	161,846	$735.7
Furnace fans	33,193	$252.0	54,008	$178.4
All retrofit types	1,124,848	$9,446.3	594,234	$5,764.8

Source: GAO analysis of IRS data.

These tax returns account for about 25 percent of all claimants and about 59 percent of total spending in 2009. Because of the overall credit limit, their credit claimed is less than 30 percent of their spending and is around 49 percent of all credit claimed.

31

Appendix II: Use of the Nonbusiness Energy Property Credit

Table 3: Use of the Nonbusiness Energy Property Credit by Claimants with Limited Tax Liability in 2009

Retrofit type	Claimants reporting spending on only one type of retrofit		Claimants reporting spending on more than one type of retrofit	
	Number	Spending (in millions)	Number	Spending (in millions)
Insulation	37,837	$118.5	70,361	$118.1
Windows	77,150	$405.5	90,071	$254.5
Doors	29,645	$52.7	82,309	$94.9
Roofs	28,871	$166.9	34,955	$120.0
Energy efficient building property	52,861	$276.0	34,693	$95.4
Furnaces and hot water boilers	66,366	$296.8	30,112	$54.6
Furnace fans	11,592	$56.9	14,434	$30.0
All retrofit types	304,322	$1,373.3	142,698	$767.7

Source: GAO analysis of IRS data.

These tax returns account for about 7 percent of all claimants and about 8 percent of total spending in 2009. Because of limited tax liability, their credit claimed is less than 30 percent of their spending and equals about 5 percent of all credit claimed.

32

GAO's Mission	The Government Accountability Office, the audit, evaluation, and investigative arm of Congress, exists to support Congress in meeting its constitutional responsibilities and to help improve the performance and accountability of the federal government for the American people. GAO examines the use of public funds; evaluates federal programs and policies; and provides analyses, recommendations, and other assistance to help Congress make informed oversight, policy, and funding decisions. GAO's commitment to good government is reflected in its core values of accountability, integrity, and reliability.
Obtaining Copies of GAO Reports and Testimony	The fastest and easiest way to obtain copies of GAO documents at no cost is through GAO's website (www.gao.gov). Each weekday afternoon, GAO posts on its website newly released reports, testimony, and correspondence. To have GAO e-mail you a list of newly posted products, go to www.gao.gov and select "E-mail Updates."
Order by Phone	The price of each GAO publication reflects GAO's actual cost of production and distribution and depends on the number of pages in the publication and whether the publication is printed in color or black and white. Pricing and ordering information is posted on GAO's website, http://www.gao.gov/ordering.htm. Place orders by calling (202) 512-6000, toll free (866) 801-7077, or TDD (202) 512-2537. Orders may be paid for using American Express, Discover Card, MasterCard, Visa, check, or money order. Call for additional information.
Connect with GAO	Connect with GAO on Facebook, Flickr, Twitter, and YouTube. Subscribe to our RSS Feeds or E-mail Updates. Listen to our Podcasts. Visit GAO on the web at www.gao.gov.
To Report Fraud, Waste, and Abuse in Federal Programs	Contact: Website: www.gao.gov/fraudnet/fraudnet.htm E-mail: fraudnet@gao.gov Automated answering system: (800) 424-5454 or (202) 512-7470
Congressional Relations	Katherine Siggerud, Managing Director, siggerudk@gao.gov, (202) 512-4400, U.S. Government Accountability Office, 441 G Street NW, Room 7125, Washington, DC 20548
Public Affairs	Chuck Young, Managing Director, youngc1@gao.gov, (202) 512-4800 U.S. Government Accountability Office, 441 G Street NW, Room 7149 Washington, DC 20548

Please Print on Recycled Paper.